READ RON
Rondeau, Amanda, 1974-
-Ock as in block

D1272941

DATE DUE

JUL 2 6 2005		
AUG 1 6 2005		
OCT 1 2 2005		
JUL 1 8 2006		
MAR 3 1 2008		
AUG 0 5 2008		
MAR 0 4 2009		
JUL 0 7 2009		
SEP 0 1 2009		
AUG 0 3 2010		
AUG 1 7 2010		
GAYLORD		PRINTED IN U.S.A.

SandCastle

Word Families Set 5

-ock as in block

Amanda Rondeau

Consulting Editor Monica Marx, M.A./Reading Specialist

ABDO
Publishing Company

Published by SandCastle™, an imprint of ABDO Publishing Company, 4940 Viking Drive, Edina, Minnesota 55435.

Copyright © 2003 by Abdo Consulting Group, Inc. International copyrights reserved in all countries. No part of this book may be reproduced in any form without written permission from the publisher. SandCastle™ is a trademark and logo of ABDO Publishing Company.

Printed in the United States.

Credits
Edited by: Pam Price
Curriculum Coordinator: Nancy Tuminelly
Cover and Interior Design and Production: Mighty Media
Photo Credits: Comstock, Corbis Images, Hemera, PhotoDisc, Rubberball Productions

Library of Congress Cataloging-in-Publication Data

Rondeau, Amanda, 1974-
    -Ock as in block / Amanda Rondeau.
      p. cm. -- (Word families. Set V)
    Summary: Introduces, in brief text and illustrations, the use of the letter combination "ock" in such words as "block," "clock," "knock," and "shamrock."
    ISBN 1-59197-250-7
    1. Readers (Primary) [1. Vocabulary. 2. Reading.] I. Title.

PE1119 .R694 2003
428.1--dc21

2002038226

SandCastle™ books are created by a professional team of educators, reading specialists, and content developers around five essential components that include phonemic awareness, phonics, vocabulary, text comprehension, and fluency. All books are written, reviewed, and leveled for guided reading, early intervention reading, and Accelerated Reader® programs and designed for use in shared, guided, and independent reading and writing activities to support a balanced approach to literacy instruction.

Let Us Know

After reading the book, SandCastle would like you to tell us your stories about reading. What is your favorite page? Was there something hard that you needed help with? Share the ups and downs of learning to read. We want to hear from you! To get posted on the ABDO Publishing Company Web site, send us e-mail at:

sandcastle@abdopub.com

SandCastle Level: Transitional

GYPSUM PUBLIC LIBRARY
P.O. BOX 979   48 LUNDGREN BLVD.
GYPSUM, CO 81637 (970) 524-5080

-ock Words

block

clock

crock

dock

rock

sock

There is the letter *B* on
this block.

The tower has a big clock.

Don is making a crock
out of clay.

Tina and Jack fish on the dock.

The Green family rests
near a big rock.

Beth is putting on a
sock.

The Giant Shamrock

There once was a giant
shamrock.

It grew very tall
near a rock.

The birds on the block
loved the shamrock.

It was their favorite place
to meet as a flock.

One day a strong wind
came to the block.

thud!

It blew the shamrock
down with a knock.

The birds were in shock.

They met with Brock,
the wise peacock.

"Let us fly in a flock
and lift the shamrock,"
said Brock.

They met at the rock.

Together they lifted the giant shamrock!

GYPSUM PUBLIC LIBRARY
P.O. BOX 979   48 LUNDGREN BLVD.
21 GYPSUM, CO 81637   (970) 524-5080

The -ock Word Family

block	lock
Brock	mock
clock	peacock
crock	rock
dock	shamrock
flock	shock
jock	sock
knock	stock

Glossary

Some of the words in this list may have more than one meaning. The meaning listed here reflects the way the word is used in the book.

crock   a clay pot or container

favorite   something you like most of all

knock   to hit something with force and make it fall

peacock   a large male bird known for its blue and green tail feathers that can be spread into a fan shape

shamrock   a small, green plant with three leaves that is the national symbol of Ireland

About SandCastle™

A professional team of educators, reading specialists, and content developers created the SandCastle™ series to support young readers as they develop reading skills and strategies and increase their general knowledge. The SandCastle™ series has four levels that correspond to early literacy development in young children. The levels are provided to help teachers and parents select the appropriate books for young readers.

Emerging Readers
(no flags)

Beginning Readers
(1 flag)

Transitional Readers
(2 flags)

Fluent Readers
(3 flags)

These levels are meant only as a guide. All levels are subject to change.

To see a complete list of SandCastle™ books and other nonfiction titles from ABDO Publishing Company, visit www.abdopub.com or contact us at:

4940 Viking Drive, Edina, Minnesota 55435 • 1-800-800-1312 • fax: 1-952-831-1632